j577.4   Pipes, Rose.
p
          Grasslands.

$22.11

DATE			

GRASSLANDS

Rose Pipes

RAINTREE
STECK-VAUGHN
P U B L I S H E R S
The Steck-Vaughn Company

Austin, Texas

Published by Raintree Steck-Vaughn Publishers, an imprint of Steck-Vaughn Company

A ZOË BOOK

Editors: Kath Davies, Pam Wells
Design & Production: Sterling Associates
Map: Sterling Associates

Library of Congress Cataloging-in-Publication Data

Pipes, Rose.
   Grasslands / Rose Pipes.
      p. cm. — (World Habitats)
   "A Zoë Book"—T.p. verso.
   Includes index.
   Summary: Introduces some notable grasslands around the world, including the Argentinian pampas, the North American prairie, and the Australian grasslands.
   ISBN 0-8172-5005-0
   1. Grasslands—Juvenile literature. [1. Grasslands.] I. Title.
  II. Series: Pipes, Rose. World habitats.
  QH541.5.P7P57
  577.4—dc21
                                    97-9073
                                          CIP
                                          AC

Printed in Italy
Bound in the United States
1 2 3 4 5 6 7 8 9   01 00 99 98   97

Photographic acknowledgments

The publishers wish to acknowledge, with thanks, the following photographic sources:

Environmental Images / Clive Jones 27; Robert Harding Picture Library / Explorer 21; The Hutchison Library 9 / Michael Kahn 6; / Robert Francis 10; / Vanessa Boeye 14; / Stephen Pern 15; Impact Photos / Neil Morrison 5; / John Cole 13; / Alain Le Garsmeur 16; / Javed A Jafferji 26; South American Pictures / Tony Morrison 18, 19, 20; Still Pictures / M & C Denis-Huot - cover background, 28; / Klein/Hubert - cover inset bl, 23; / Brigitte Marcon - cover inset tl; / Stephen Pern - title page, 17; / Hjalte Tin 7; / Mark Edwards 8; / Mikkel Ostergaard 25; TRIP / L Reemer 29; Zefa 11, 12, 22, 24.

The publishers have made every effort to trace the copyright holders, but if they have inadvertently overlooked any, they will be pleased to make the necessary arrangement at the first opportunity.

Contents

All the words that appear in **bold** are explained in the Glossary on page 30.

What and Where Are Grasslands?

NORTH
AMERICA

Mongolian
grasslands

EUROPE

The Prairie

ASIA

Tropic of Cancer

AFRICA

Equator

SOUTH
AMERICA

Tanzanian
grasslands

Australian
grasslands

Tropic of Capricorn

The Pampas

AUSTRALIA

Key

Prairies and steppes

Savanna

ANTARCTICA

The map shows two kinds of grasslands.

Grasslands called savannas are in warm, dry lands. Grasslands called prairies, or steppes (steps), are in cooler lands.

There may be no rain on the savanna for many months. Rain falls for part or most of the year in the prairies.

Wild grasses grow in parts of the world where it is too dry for forests to grow and too wet for deserts to form. These grasses often grow in places that are flooded for part of the year.

This hippopotamus lives in Kenya, Africa. It eats the grass that is growing near the water.

Plants and Animals

Grasslands are often flat places with few or no trees. The animals who live there have **adapted** to life in the grasslands. Many animals can run very fast across the flat

Some birds use grass to make their nests. You can see a weaver bird's nest in this picture.

land. Some animals make holes, or burrows, to hide in under the ground.

The soils and the weather on prairies and steppes are good for growing **cereal crops**. Wheat, corn, and barley are cereals. Their seeds, or grains, are crushed to make flour. Then the flour is used for making bread.

There are sheep and cattle farms on many grasslands. Meat, wool, milk, cheese, and yogurt are all important grassland **products**.

The farmland in this picture is in Estonia. Hundreds of years ago, most farmland was wild grassland. Now it may be an important area for growing crops.

In the savanna the weather and the soils are not as good for growing crops as they are on the prairies and steppes. Here, most people herd animals.

This picture shows part of the dry savanna grasslands in Burkina Faso in West Africa. People keep animals for meat, milk, and skins.

If rain does not fall for a long time, the grass and the crops may die from heat and lack of water. Grassland fires are also a danger in very dry summers.

Some wild grassland animals are in danger because people hunt and kill them. The hunters make money by selling the animals' skins, horns, or tusks.

There are many **national parks** in the world's grasslands. Here, the animals are **protected**.

This is the Masai Mara National Park in Kenya, Africa. Oryx are grazing on the grassland.

The Prairie of North America

Wild grassland once covered a large part of the United States and Canada. The North American grassland is called the prairie. Today, there are farms on most of the prairie. On the western, dry prairie, farmers keep

This farmland is in North Dakota. You can see the huge fields where cereals, such as wheat and barley, grow. This state often has harsh winter storms.

cattle. On the wetter land in the east, crops grow well.

For hundreds of years, the prairie was home to Native Americans and to millions of buffalo and other wild animals.

About 150 years ago, people from Europe came to farm the prairie. The new settlers wanted the land for themselves. They killed the buffalo and drove away the Native Americans. There are still some buffalo living on the prairie, but they only live in national parks.

Buffalo are protected in national parks. These buffalo are in Wind Cave National Park in South Dakota.

When farming changed the grassland
habitat, many wild animals lost their food
and their homes. Wild grasses and other
plants were plowed up. However, some wild
animals still live on the prairies.

These prairie dogs live on the prairies. They make
burrows in the ground. Like rabbits and coyotes,
they eat grasses and cereals.

In the driest parts of the prairies, rain may not fall for many months. The soil dries out and turns into dust. These areas are called **dustbowls**. If there are strong winds, they will blow away the dust, and the soil will be lost forever.

If the fields are on sloping ground, the farmers plow the soil around the slopes, not up and down. This helps to stop rain from washing away the soil.

Prairie farmers now plant trees around their fields. The trees shelter the land from strong winds. Tree roots help to keep the soil in place.

This field in central Kansas is on sloping ground. You can see that the farmer has plowed around the slopes.

The Grasslands of Mongolia

No trees grow on the flat, high grasslands, or steppes, of Mongolia. It is a hard place to live. Food is not plentiful here for people or for animals.

In summer it is very hot on these steppes, but the winters are bitterly cold, and snow may fall. The animals you can see are goats and yaks. Yaks are a type of cattle. They provide milk, skins, and meat.

Some people who live on the Mongolian steppes keep herds of animals. These herders are **nomads**. They move around to find food for their animals.

The herders live in round tents called **yurts**. A stove inside the yurt is used for cooking and heating. A thick woolen cloth called felt covers the wooden poles to form a **shelter**. The hole in the middle of the roof is for a chimney.

These herders have just milked their goats. The woman is carrying the milk in a pail to her yurt.

The herders use milk from their animals to make foods, such as cheese and yogurt. They buy other foods in the towns, where they sell animal skins, meat, wool, and horses. Horses are very important. Some families may own as many as sixty horses.

A Mongolian herder with his horses

Nearly half the people of Mongolia live and work on **ranches**, or farms, in the grasslands. In the driest parts the ranchlands are in danger of turning into desert.

Large numbers of ranch animals are eating the grass and wearing away the soil on the steppes. When the grass has gone, there is nothing to hold down, or anchor, the soil. It turns into dust that the strong winds blow away easily.

You can see the grassland near the river in this picture. But on the higher ground the land is sandy desert.

The Pampas of Argentina

The Spanish people who settled in Argentina called the land the "pampas." The soils of the pampas are rich, and plenty of rain falls on them. It is good land for farming.

The pampas are wide flat lands on the east side of the country. People began to farm the pampas about 400 years ago. Before that time, the land was a huge sea of wild grasses. Wolves with manes once lived in the wild grasslands.

Today, farmers grow cereals and other crops in the wetter parts of the pampas. Cattle and sheep graze on large ranches in the drier areas.

When the farmers grew crops, the wolves' habitat changed. Maned wolves, like this one, moved to live in the woodlands of southern Brazil.

The rhea is the largest bird in South America. It is well adapted to living on wide open grasslands. It eats grass and other plants, as well as insects and small **mammals**. It cannot fly, but it can run very fast.

Cowboys, called "gauchos" in Spanish, used to live and work on the pampas. They rode horses to round up cattle and sheep on the ranches. Very few gauchos work on the pampas today. But there are still **festivals** when cowboys dress up as gauchos.

Cowboys dressed as gauchos ride horses at gaucho festivals.

The Grasslands of Australia

Nearly half of the land in Australia is desert. Most of the rest of the land is grassland. The hills of earth in this Australian grassland are the nests of insects called termites.

In some of the wildest areas, the grassland habitat has not changed for thousands of years. Many wild animals still live in these natural areas.

The kangaroo is one of the largest wild animals living in the Australian grasslands. Kangaroos eat grass and other plants.

Young kangaroos grow inside a pouch, or pocket, on their mother's body. Animals with pouches are called **marsupials**. Most of the world's marsupials live in Australia.

Kangaroos leap across the ground on their long back legs.

When the European settlers came to Australia, they brought sheep and cattle with them to graze on the grasslands. Sheep farms in Australia are called sheep stations.

Most of the sheep in Australia are merinos, like these sheep. Merino sheep are famous for their fine wool. This wool is now **exported**, or sent, to countries all over the world.

Until about 200 years ago, the only people in Australia were the **Aborigines**, the native people. They lived a nomadic life on the grasslands. They hunted wild animals and gathered berries and plants to eat.

The European settlers treated these people very badly. Many Aborigines died or were moved off the land.

Today, most Aborigines live in or near towns and cities. A few still work on farms in the country.

This Aboriginal family lives on a farm. Some Aborigines now own land in the countryside.

The Grasslands of Tanzania

The Masai people are cattle herders who live on the East African savanna. Their lands are in Kenya and Tanzania. The Masai live in groups on small areas of land.

Masai women milk the cows. The children help to herd the cattle.

In the dry season, the Masai move around the grasslands with their cattle. They travel a long way to find grass for their cattle to eat.

Thorn trees and wild grasses grow on the savanna in Tanzania. There are very few farms here, so the wild grassland habitat has not changed much.

Millions of wild animals and birds live on the savanna. Many of the animals are grass eaters.

Zebra and wildebeests graze on the Serengeti Plain in Tanzania.

About a quarter of Tanzania's land is in national parks. Thousands of tourists visit Tanzania's national parks to see the wildlife. Zebras, wildebeests, and cheetahs are just some of the animals there.

Many of the larger mammals, such as this cheetah, eat meat. They run fast to catch their **prey**, or food.

Tourists pay to travel in the national parks. The money is used to take care of the parks. It also helps to pay for people to study the wildlife there.

More than 3 million mammals live in the Serengeti National Park. The world's largest bird, the ostrich, lives here too. Although it cannot fly, it can run fast.

These tourists are taking photographs in the Serengeti National Park. People can drive close to the animals, but it is not safe to walk around.

Glossary

Aborigines: The people first known to have lived in Australia.

adapted: If a plant or an animal can find everything it needs to live in a place, we say that it has adapted to that place. The animals can find food and shelter, and the plants have enough food in the soil and enough water. Some animals have changed their shape or their color over a long time, so that they can catch food or hide easily. Some plants in dry areas can store water in their stems or roots.

cereals: Grain crops such as wheat, corn, barley, and rice. The cereals we eat for breakfast are made from these grain crops.

crops: Plants that farmers grow to use or to sell.

dustbowl: An area of land where wild grasses were plowed up. Then the soil dried into dust.

exported: Sold and taken to another country.

festival: A time when people remember something special in the past, or a special time of the year.

habitat: The natural home of a plant or animal. Examples of habitats are deserts, forests, and grasslands.

mammals: The group of animals whose young feed on their mother's milk.

marsupials: Animals that carry their young in a pouch. The young feed on their mother's milk.

national parks: Laws are passed to protect these lands and their wildlife from harm. National parks are usually places with beautiful scenery and rare wildlife.

nomads: People who do not live in one place. They move around all the time. Nomads in desert areas usually live in tents.

prey: An animal that another animal hunts for food.

products: Crops that we grow or goods that we make.

protected: Kept safe from changes that would damage the habitat.

ranches: Large farms where farmers keep cattle, sheep, or other animals.

shelter: A place one goes to for protection from wind, rain, and cold. A shelter is also a safe place.

yurt: A round tent that is used by nomads for shelter or protection. Like most tents, it is easy to move from place to place.

Index